TO TIM

power for the church in the midst of chaos

Harry N. Huxhold

Publishing House
St. Louis London

Concordia Publishing House, St. Louis, Missouri
Concordia Publishing House Ltd., London, E. C. 1

Library of Congress Catalog Card No. 73-82078
ISBN 0-570-03160-5

MANUFACTURED IN THE UNITED STATES OF AMERICA

INTRODUCTION

Ministry in any urban parish forces pastor and people to struggle to reassess their task and purpose in their evangelical mission. The confused environs of the changed community and the chaotic atmosphere of tortured times in the world, the nation, and the church have not been conducive to high morale in the congregation.

The consistent criticisms that have been leveled at the church from within and without have disturbed, frustrated, and wearied the faithful who would like to find hope "for such a time as this." And hope there is. The apostolic faith is a fervent witness to the fact that, as pessimism grows in the world, Christians have every right to assert their optimistic faith in God who rules over all. These meditations are reflections on the power that was available to the apostolic church, which is our model for hope.

There are features of the life of the apostolic church analogous to those of the contemporary church. We pray that these meditations will help the reader discover that the power and resources of God's Spirit are no less available to the church now than then.

Harry N. Huxhold

CONTENTS

power *in Language*

When the day of Pentecost had come, they were all together in one place. And suddenly a sound came from heaven like the rush of a mighty wind, and it filled all the house where they were sitting. And there appeared to them tongues as of fire, distributed and resting on each one of them. And they were all filled with the Holy Spirit and began to speak in other tongues, as the Spirit gave them utterance.

Now there were dwelling in Jerusalem Jews, devout men from every nation under heaven. And at this sound the multitude came together, and they were bewildered, because each one heard them speaking his own language. And they were amazed and wondered, saying, "Are not all these who are speaking Galileans? And how is it that we hear, each of us in his own native language? Parthians and Medes and Elamites and residents of Mesopotamia, Judea and Cappadocia, Pontus and Asia, Phrygia and Pamphylia, Egypt and the parts of Libya belonging to Cyrene, and visitors from Rome, both Jews and proselytes, Cretans and Arabians, we hear them telling in our own tongues the mighty works of God." And all were amazed and perplexed, saying to one another, "What does this mean?" But others mocking said, "They are filled with new wine."

Acts 2:1-13

POWER in Language

Our celebration of Pentecost is the celebration of the great work of the Holy Spirit. What the company of the faithful followers of the Lord Jesus Christ observed on the first Pentecost was the power of God's Spirit to create faith in the hearts of men. This is a mighty act of God no less magnificent or dramatic than any other act of God. In doing this work God enables man to do the impossible, for Scripture plainly teaches the reality that no man can say that Jesus is Lord but by the Holy Ghost. It is still so. Therefore when we hear someone confess the Lord Jesus Christ, God continues the work of Pentecost and we are witnesses to the mighty act of God. Our hearts should be filled with joy as we celebrate this day and acknowledge that the Holy Spirit is still let loose among us. We should take this occasion to make it indelibly clear that the Spirit is among us. That is the purpose of this account of the first Pentecost in the Book of Acts. Luke wanted to give the full evidence that the Holy Spirit worked plainly and clearly in the lives of people as He brought them to faith in Jesus as both Lord and Christ. Out of many languages He made clear one Word, and He gave power to its language.

Luke indicates that there were many people who had come to Jerusalem to celebrate the Jewish Feast of Pentecost. Because the Jews had been dispersed throughout the world, these people came from many lands and spoke different languages. It is doubtful that many of them spoke

Hebrew, though most of them probably did know the language that was popular throughout the world of that day the Koine, that is, common Greek. But before we speak of the many languages, it is worthwhile to stop and reflect on the gift of language itself. The root word for language is from the Latin *lingua,* tongue. What a blessing it is that we can use the tongue to make distinguishable sounds that we call language! Our ability to do so is plainly a wondrous gift from our Creator God. When men try to explain the gift of language, they are forced to concede that it is not only a marvel but a mystery. Many theories have been advanced to explain the origin of language, but no matter how elaborate the explanation, we have to bow before the fact that language is a special gift. By faith we discern that it is a special gift from God by which we are able to communicate with regard to our emotions, our needs, our worship, and our vocation. That we are so endowed enables us to engage ourselves in the business of living in a way that lesser creatures within the creation are not able.

But why are there many languages and dialects in the earth? Differences in language and dialects are definite barriers and hindrances in the business of communications among people who want to live and talk together. Scholars who study man and his language are not too clear on this point. They can find some similarities in the families of languages, but there are languages which show no relationships whatsoever. In the Scriptures we have the ancient account of the Tower of Babel. You will recall that the story indicates that men abandoned their project of building a tower that would reach into the heavens. They gave up this effort because God confused their language and they could not understand one another. What happened? We do not have the details, and we do not know how the confusion actually manifested itself. However, the story is clear on one point. The confusion of language was a judgment on man for his pride. It is pride that alienates and separates men from one another. It is the pride of man that erects barriers between men and makes them unable to communicate. One can sense this as he travels in foreign countries where people may use and know the language of the tourists but refuse to engage in conversation or offer help by hiding behind the barrier of their language. The Old Testament is consistent in making this observation about differences in language. Men were recognized as being essentially different when they spoke another language. They were strange and alien to one another. And do we not have to ask: Are not the differences cultivated and protected by men because they in their pride want to be different from one another?

How important it is that we then strive to overcome the pride that divides men! We must look for those means by which we can get people to reason together, to speak together, and to dialog with one another. We can begin by exploring the similarities of language. One way of teaching a new language today is to start the beginner out with the words that he already knows from another language. There have been attempts at creating a world language. We know how missionaries have worked with pidgin English. There have been efforts to create a language for diplomatic purposes. The great spread of English-speaking people through the growth of the British Empire in the last century, and the world wars of this century, have so popularized English that it has become almost a world language. People who live in the proximity of other people speaking different languages of necessity often develop good language facility. One can take a tour in Europe to hear a guide give tour explanations in up to seven different languages. However, in spite of the hopeful signs of speaking as one people, we still see men unable to communicate even when they speak the same tongue. Pride still keeps them apart.

We are dreadfully conscious of the problem of communication in our time. Some people hold that the older generation is totally incapable of communicating with the young. Others believe that we cannot have meaningful dialog between the races. You can add as many different kinds of groups as you want—churches, labor and management, and the like. Again the problem is always the same. It is not simply the language that is the problem for man. It is his pride. The Scriptures once more have a realistic view of the problem. The Old Testament view of man pictured a man's tongue as the instrument of his heart. So also our Lord made it clear that it was not what came out of a man's mouth that defiled him, but what came out of his heart.

It is not surprising then that in order to rescue man from the perils of his own language, God Himself would have to speak to man. This is what God chose to do through His Son Jesus Christ, our Lord. Jesus is called the Word of God. He is the incarnate Word of God, the Word of God become flesh. What in His gracious love God revealed under His promises and the offices of prophets, priests, and kings, that He now revealed more fully in His Son. The lessons He taught in His great and mighty acts, through His spokesmen the prophets, His servants the priests, and His rulers the kings, were not always clear. He now spoke much more intelligibly and dramatically. In Jesus God gave the clearest and best expression to man that He could.

What was it that God spoke to us through His Son? He spoke a language of judgment and of love. In Jesus God demonstrated His wrath as He permitted His Son to be the victim of man's hatred. Those who put Him to death heard His language—His words and His message. But they would not believe. It was not because they did not understand. It was because they would not trust His Word. Therefore Jesus was put to death for man's sin, on account of man's sin, or as a result of man's sin. But the incarnate Word was not to be hushed. God raised His Son, saying most clearly to the world that in this Son there was life and hope for all of the world. Pentecost was the day when the disciples by the gift of God's Spirit awoke to the implications of all that this meant, and they broke into the streets to tell all Jerusalem what the consequences were of the death of Jesus Christ. All Jerusalem could not know that the city that had put Jesus to death could now be brought to life through this same Christ. And those who formerly could not understand could now discern in the languages of the disciples the Word of God. "We hear them telling in our own tongues the mighty works of God." What was important was not that they heard their own language, but that with the heart they could hear and believe the mighty works of God.

That is the most important sign, miracle, wonder, marvel—call it what you will—of all. By the gift of God's Spirit we can hear and know the works of God and believe them because of our Lord Jesus Christ. May we never forget that! Through all of the ranting, shouting, polarizing, and debating that goes on in life, may we always hear clearly and intelligibly the love language which our God speaks to us through our Lord Jesus Christ! As though there were not enough problems to cause disharmony and disunity among men today, even within the church, we discover people who believe that they should cause Christians to be at odds with one another. Whenever that happens, then ask, "Can we hear in our own tongues the mighty works of God?" If we cannot hear the clear, plain, and intelligible witness to the fact that God has redeemed us through the Lord Jesus Christ, then we have every right to hold those suspect who pretend to speak in the name of our God. We are bombarded on all sides by all kinds of voices, languages, philosophies, and ideas. We must engage ourselves in worship and the study of God's Word so that we are equipped always to hear and recognize the Gospel of our Lord Jesus Christ.

What the Pentecost story means to us then is that God has reversed the disorder of Babel. The judgment that had separated men because of their pride has now been overcome by the singular language of love which God has spoken to us in Jesus Christ. Strangely enough, it was within one generation that the church was thrown into disorder at Corinth by the confusion over the gift of tongues, that phenomenon by which men are able to speak ecstatic language. This is a phenomenon which is again quite prevalent in Christendom and has been causing considerable disunity. Paul's advice at that time is advice that we should follow whenever this kind of divisiveness threatens us. He urged that men not covet that gift, but rather that they should earnestly strive to express themselves in love, even as our God spoke plainly to us of His love in Jesus Christ. There is no reason for us to live with any kind of communications gap among ourselves or be frustrated by the world's inability to carry on dialog. We are sent to speak reconciliation. We celebrate the miracle of God's love in Jesus Christ as by the power of the Spirit He enables us to speak and live by His love.

power *in Sermons*

"Brethren, I may say to you confidently of the patriarch David that he both died and was buried, and his tomb is with us to this day. Being therefore a prophet, and knowing that God had sworn with an oath to him that He would set one of his descendants upon his throne, he foresaw and spoke of the resurrection of the Christ, that He was not abandoned to Hades, nor did His flesh see corruption. This Jesus God raised up, and of that we all are witnesses. Being therefore exalted at the right hand of God, and having received from the Father the promise of the Holy Spirit, He has poured out this which you see and hear. For David did not ascend into the heavens; but he himself says,

" 'The Lord said to my Lord, Sit at My right hand, till I make Thy enemies a stool for Thy feet.'

"Let all the house of Israel therefore know assuredly that God has made Him both Lord and Christ, this Jesus whom you crucified."

Now when they heard this they were cut to the heart, and said to Peter and the rest of the apostles, "Brethren, what shall we do?" And Peter said to them, "Repent, and be baptized every one of you in the name of Jesus Christ for the forgiveness of your sins; and you shall receive the gift of the Holy Spirit. For the promise is to you and to your children and to all that are far off, every one whom the Lord our God calls to Him."

Acts 2:29-39

POWER
in Sermons

Remember the flood of how-to books that appeared on the bookstands some years ago? One such book was Aaron Copland's helpful little manual *What to Listen for in Music.* If someone asked you to tell him what to listen for in a sermon, what would you answer? Perhaps that is an unfair question, because you may not have thought too much about the matter. But suppose some stranger or friend were interested in accepting your invitation to go to church with you and then asked you the question, "What should I listen for in the sermon?" You would have to give some kind of answer. Then again you may have some definite ideas on what you expect to hear in the sermon. Some people may like to hear the stories or illustrations the preacher uses. Others may be listening for an element of surprise. Still others may be paying special attention to the language. Some of the children (and I suppose a good many adults) may be listening for the Amen. Some may be listening for the way in which the Word is applied to current events. Some like a topical sermon rather than an explanation or exposition of the Scripture. Some come to be comforted by the sermon. Some like the fire-and-brimstone sermon. All this kind of listening goes on every Sunday morning. We know that it does, because people have told us so. There are many kinds of listeners, but really there is only one central message. That central message should be the power of the sermon.

The sermon is the exercise in which both the listeners and the preacher work together to hear what God through His Holy Spirit would speak to them. As they work together to determine from the Word what it is that God would speak to them, they should be pretty well agreed on what it is that they are working at. One of my students at the University of Minnesota came to my office to talk to me about my sermons. He said that they were quite different from what he was used to at home. I asked him what he heard at home. He said that the minister thundered at them regularly about sending their children to the parochial school and about drinking beer. He said the people were used to sitting back and saying, "Here he goes again!" I asked if the people obeyed what he said. His answer was no. The sermon in that congregation was a kind of game which the people and pastor played. It was a verbal spanking that made no difference to anyone. But if the sermon is not to be just a Sunday morning game or mental exercise, what must it be? What is it that we are working on together? What must be the goal of preaching and listening?

One would think that the answer is quite obvious. We should be listening for the Word of God. But the problem is that the Word is so easily abused and misinterpreted. How are the listeners to know that they have heard the Word of God or not? Then there is this large variety of expectations on the part of the hearers. How can the preacher feel that he has reached the audience? Then we also know that there are so many different approaches to preaching and so many styles. How can the congregations know they have heard a proper treatment of the text? Those questions have been seriously entertained by many students of preaching. Very much has been written as to what should make for effective listening and preaching. Every great preacher who comes along thinks he should write a book about it. But perhaps one of the most effective studies of the matter is a little book by an English Biblical scholar by the name of C. H. Dodd. Dr. Dodd reasoned that if we are to be faithful to the Christian task of preaching, then we ought to examine carefully the models we have for preaching in the New Testament. He did just that. His little book, *The Apostolic Preaching,* is an analysis of the sermons and the preaching of the apostles. He examined the sermons particularly of Peter and Paul. One of the sermons is our text for today. It is a part of the sermon which Peter preached at Pentecost. It is a good example of what we can study to determine what we should listen for in a sermon.

Peter's Pentecostal sermon contains those basic elements which Dr. Dodd discovered were consistently present in the apostolic witness. Paul wrote to the Corinthians, "It pleased God by the foolishness of the preaching to save them that believe" (1 Cor. 1:21). The Greek word for preaching here is *kerygma.* The *kerygma* is the preacher's message. The word comes from *keryssein,* to proclaim. A *keryx* is a town crier, an auctioneer, a herald, or anyone who lifts up his voice to call attention to an important announcement. The *kerygma* of God is an announcement by which He saves men. That announcement has definite ingredients which comprise the saving message of God. Preaching does not depend on clever words or words of wisdom, Paul noted. Rather, preaching is effective in the hearts of men because it is faithful to the witness of something that God wants proclaimed to stir and win the hearts of men. Peter's sermon on Pentecost was structured to set forth this *kerygma.* In the sermon we will find six major points that set forth for us what it is that our God has done and is doing to bring us into relationship with Himself.

What is striking about the sermonic material in the Book of Acts is that it agrees so substantially with the material in Paul. We are quite certain that Paul began his preaching and writing much earlier than the writing of the Book of Acts. So this brings us to the reassuring conclusion that from the very beginning the disciples gave their consistent witness to the meaning of the events in the life of our Lord. The same, of course, is true of the heart of the material in the gospels written by the evangelists. You say, "Well, that ought to be perfectly obvious. Why even bring the matter up?" In answer we have to say that it has not always been so obvious to everyone, unfortunately. But that is not our main reason for introducing it here. The point is that if the apostles and evangelists were so careful to maintain a consistency in heralding the *kerygma,* should we not also do the same? Would we have the right to ignore their efforts by choosing to shape our preaching and listening according to our own fancy? Would we in the face of the Scriptural witness have the privilege to superimpose on the *kerygma* our own ideas of what the goals of sermonizing should be? The answer to the question: "What should I listen for in a sermon?" is already prescribed for us by what the *kerygma* is. The stories and illustrations, the language, the length, the form, whether the sermon is topical or expository, these are not the important factors. The importance of the sermon is tied to the *kerygma* itself.

What are the points contained in the *kerygma?* Dr. Dodd found these points in the sermons of Acts. First, the age of fulfillment has dawned. Second, the fulfillment has taken place through the ministry, death, and resurrection of Jesus Christ. Third, when God raised His Son Jesus from the dead, He exalted Him at His right hand to be both Lord and Christ. Fourth, the Holy Spirit, whom God has bestowed upon His church, is the sign of Christ's continuing presence and power among us. Fifth, God will complete His kingly work among us with the Second Advent of our Lord. Finally, the *kerygma* closes with an appeal for repentance on the part of the hearers and the promise of the salvation which God offers us through the Lord Jesus Christ. Now certainly this *kerygma* was presented in a variety of ways, but the essential ingredients were there. This means there is only one *kerygma,* one sermon. The approaches and style may be different, but the message remains the same. Some people do not like to hear that. That sounds too monotonous. The temptation for the preacher and the hearers is to look for something novel, something flashy. I recall from my work in the stationery and bookstore during my seminary days that we always had a pretty good sale of the book, *Snappy Sermon Starters.* People look for the sensational. Yet that is not what we need. We must look for the *kerygma.*

Now lest you think that the preaching of the *kerygma* is monotonous and dreary, dry and uninteresting, let me remind you how dreadfully monotonous the news of the world is. Essentially all the news media – radio, TV, and the newspapers – report to you the same message every day. They tell you that man is evil, that he is subject to judgment, and that his worst enemy is death. That news is as old as man. Yet we are curiously drawn to the repetitious details of how the evil of man manifests itself every day. You have heard repeatedly that the real radicals in the community and on college campuses are a small percentage of the total population, yet they command all the attention. They do so because we have this insatiable appetite for bad news. No matter how often we read or hear the bad news, somehow the news media are convinced that this is the only kind of news that people want. The *kerygma* is God's news, the good news for us that God has completely reversed the values of the world, that He has destroyed the power of the devil, that He has overcome our adversaries for us. The *kerygma* is not a call to battle but the proclamation that the battle has been won. The *kerygma* is absolutely the best news that we can hear for our condition and situation. The *kerygma* announces to us the fact that by repentance and faith we can be incorporated into the eternal goodness of the Father.

What we are to listen for in a sermon then is the setting forth of Jesus Christ as our only means of achieving whatever the specific goal of a particular sermon might be. We can take any goal that we will and Jesus Christ will always be the means by which we are able to attain it. We must also recognize that the *kerygma* is always a call to repentance and faith. The very offer which God makes assumes our sinful condition. At the same time the offer also holds out to us the radical solution to our problem, namely, that by His grace God is able to change us and convert us into His saints. This leaves us with the freedom to preach about any subject, to direct our prayerful and careful attention to it. We have the freedom to prepare and preach the sermon and to listen to it in the particular manner we choose. However, we shall always look for that central message which says that Jesus is our Savior and Redeemer. At Jerusalem that day, when Peter preached his sermon, there were many men, but the *kerygma* proclaimed to them that there was this one and only God who in Jesus Christ was alone their hope. So we reaffirm that the *kerygma* in this day of confusion among men remains as the only hope. By our faith alone in Him as Father, Son, and Holy Spirit—as Creator, Savior, and Sanctifier—we are saved.

power *for Blessing*

Now Peter and John were going up to the temple at the hour of prayer, the ninth hour. And a man lame from birth was being carried, whom they laid daily at that gate of the temple which is called Beautiful to ask alms of those who entered the temple. Seeing Peter and John about to go into the temple, he asked for alms. And Peter directed his gaze at him, with John, and said, "Look at us." And he fixed his attention upon them, expecting to receive something from them. But Peter said, "I have no silver and gold, but I give you what I have; in the name of Jesus Christ of Nazareth, walk." And he took him by the right hand and raised him up; and immediately his feet and ankles were made strong. And leaping up he stood and walked and entered the temple with them, walking and leaping and praising God. And all the people saw him walking and praising God, and recognized him as the one who sat for alms at the Beautiful Gate of the temple; and they were filled with wonder and amazement at what had happened to him.

Acts 3:1-10

POWER
for Blessing

The beautiful story in our text of a healing in the name of Jesus reminds us of a legend about the famous churchman St. Francis of Assisi. Francis is renowned in the history of the church for many reasons. He was instrumental in achieving some reform in the life of the church of the 13th century. He was founder of the evangelical order that bears his name. He befriended the poor and the outcasts and is fabled for his special love for birds. He himself lived a simple life, having taken the oath of poverty. In doing so he renounced the wealth that would have come to him from his affluent merchant family. His chief message to his disciples was that they were to embrace poverty so that they might serve the world in pure love and without pay. Legend has it that when he came to Rome to apply to Pope Innocent III for the right to create his order, the pope proudly showed him the splendors of Rome and the treasures of the papacy, saying, "You see, Francis, no longer can Peter say, 'Silver and gold have I none.'" Francis is reported to have replied, "But neither can he say, 'Rise up and walk.'" The legend makes its point for our day. Just when the church was showing strength and power in society, it has been seriously challenged to answer if it can still give that blessing, "Rise up and walk." In such a time as this it is good for us to ask how we may find power for blessing.

The story of the healing of the lame man at the temple gate follows closely upon the description of Pentecost and the initial development of the Pentecostal church. Peter and John went up to the temple to pray at the regular appointed hour for prayer. When a lame beggar accosted them for alms, Peter healed him in the name of Jesus. This gave Peter the opportunity to explain to the people in a sermon that it was the name of Jesus alone that had effected this marvelous healing. This was a bold testimony to the Christ who had been crucified but was now risen. This testimony led to persecution because the authorities wanted the apostles to stop speaking about Jesus or to preach in His name. The story closely parallels the ministry of our Lord Himself. For He too used the occasion of healing to preach of the love of His Father. He also was persecuted and threatened for His witness to God's love. But threats and persecution did not accomplish their purpose in either event. The name of Jesus was not to be silenced. It was a power among men, to be used among men for their blessing.

We are to see in this story that from the beginning Peter makes it clear that this great gift, the healing, came from the Lord Jesus Christ. The healing is not to be associated with the man Peter but with the name of the Lord Jesus Christ. Jesus Himself healed many people who were brought to Him in need. Peter was in this case only an instrument in His hands. And what did the healing mean but the same thing that it had meant in the ministry of Jesus? Jesus had come to let loose the power of healing among men that they might see the kingly rule of God in the world. This rule of God means that He had power over all things. But more than that, the kingly rule of God also means that by the power of His love God has broken in on those things that distort and warp His creation. The kingly rule of God means that God has reversed the judgment that fell hard upon the world. Sickness and death are the obvious signs of a fallen world, a world soiled and spoiled by sin, a world in which everything seems to go wrong. A healing in Jesus' name means that by His Messianic work Jesus redeemed fully and completely the world and the creature sinner in the world. God throttled the power of disease as evidence and a sign that He has the greater power to throttle and completely destroy the power of sin and death in our lives. This is truly the greatest gift that God could give to man.

Because it is the greatest gift which God can give to man, it was also the unexpected. The man was reconciled to his lameness. He had learned to accept it. To do so was to accept the humble if not degrading role of a beggar. He was used to asking for alms, or gifts of charity. That he should be healed was not his hope or expectation. Now, we know that there are people who are never reconciled to their misfortune. They hope against hope for some kind of deliverance from their plight. Others again are like this man in our story and accept what appears to them to be the inevitable. But regardless of how men feel about their situation, to be healed as was this man would be dramatic indeed. We are so accustomed to the power of misfortune in our lives that deep down we know that we have no right to expect release from the powers that make life miserable, no matter how much we desire freedom from them. This means that all of us fear deeply inside that the hardships we bear in this life may be a judgment from God. This is why such a story is big news. It would be today even if this man were healed in some special clinic or by some new treatment. We would today be equally enchanted by the healing in any form because we know that we have no right to expect it.

From this story we also learn something important about healing in the ministry of the church. On the one hand, we have already seen that Peter wanted everyone to understand that this was a gift of Christ. We also see that it came to the lame man as something unexpected. When we keep those facts in mind we have right to question those ministries which, purportedly carried out in the name of Christ Jesus, are great profitmaking ventures. Those who exaggerate their powers in the name of Jesus are certainly made suspect when we contrast their methods and operations with those of Peter and John in this story, or with those of our Lord Himself in the Gospel accounts. Also we are to question most seriously those who advertise that Christians have a right to expect healings. What great damage has been done to the faith because some teach that if one has faith great or large enough he should be healed! There is much healing that goes on daily in the church in the name of Jesus. It happens quietly and brings hope and courage to many. Every faithful pastor can report dramatic events of healing that take place in his ministrations. However, if he treats them in any other way than Peter does in our story, he does violence to the name of Jesus. We must all trust that the name of Jesus is still effective among us in the ministry of healing. Yet we must keep such ministry in the perspective of our story. That gives us hope and power. We do have power which is to be shared as a blessing.

Let us look again at the story to see how we can employ this power to bless many. Peter said, "I have no silver and gold." We are not to use this as an excuse when we do have silver and gold to share with those in need. God will not excuse us for being stingy with our resources when we have the capability of taking care of those in need. All of Scripture makes it clear that we are to consider the needs of our fellowmen when they are desperate and hungry. God makes it abundantly clear that we cannot be excused from our duties to look after the needs of our neighbors. Further, this story suggests something very important to us. Think of how often it is true that people are looking for something that is far less important than their real need. The lame man asked for alms and Peter gave him the power to walk. All classes of people today clamor for more money. What we really need among all men is a new sense of respect and honor. The young ask for more privileges and a greater piece of the action. What we really need to give them is the ability to mature and grow wise. The very young demand things. What we really need to give them is discipline in the things of God. The community demands taxes. What we really need to give is more than money. We need to give of ourselves to bring about reconciliation among all men.

Thus we may ask ourselves how we may render a blessing to others when they come to us for help. We are not without power. God has shared with us the powers of heaven. He has given to us of His love. He has given us hope and courage through our Lord Jesus Christ. Peter could share power in the name of Jesus because the life, death, and resurrection of Jesus Christ meant that God cared for the redemption of the world. The name of Jesus was not just a name, but it was the very power of God at work within men. We cannot hold this power to ourselves. If we do, we are the worst wasters in the world. If we try to pen up love, it becomes self-love. If we try to contain peace, it becomes inaction. If we try to sit on the Gospel, it becomes empty doctrine. We must give this power away. We can all share it, each in his own way. Some have the power to bring joy and gladness where brightness is needed. Others can share courage and hope where it is needed. Still others can bring admonition and correction when it is needed. There are many who can share beauty, vision, and endurance. No man who knows the name of Jesus Christ is bankrupt for a gift to give. All who live under the lordship and redeeming love of our Lord Jesus Christ are able to bring the resources of heaven down to earth. The power for blessing belongs to us all. Let us not neglect to use it.

One other lesson remains for us in the story. It is clear from Peter's approach that he wanted to treat the whole man. Peter did not just preach the Gospel to this man. He healed him and used the occasion of healing to testify to the Lord Jesus. So our ministry of healing cannot be one-sided. We do not believe that man's illnesses or diseases are only imagined or are the result of improper thinking. Man must be healed from what ails him. At the same time we do not think all of man's problems are only physical. Our Christian hospitals and chaplaincy programs are evidences of our attempt to deal with the whole man. So it must also be with our social ministries and our educational strategies. Our Gospel does not offer perfect health, a perfect society, or perfect life to anyone this side of the veil. But we do have the power to offer this kind of blessing in the name of Jesus, namely, that in Jesus Christ we can now enjoy an openness toward the God who created and redeemed us and who will furnish us with the necessary weapons that will enable us to meet all of our enemies and triumph over them.

power Before Men

And as they were speaking to the people, the priests and the captain of the temple and the Sadducees came upon them, annoyed because they were teaching the people and proclaiming in Jesus the resurrection from the dead. And they arrested them and put them in custody until the morrow, for it was already evening. But many of those who heard the Word believed; and the number of the men came to about five thousand.

On the morrow their rulers and elders and scribes were gathered together in Jerusalem, with Annas the high priest and Caiaphas and John and Alexander, and all who were of the high-priestly family. And when they had set them in the midst, they inquired, "By what power or by what name did you do this?" Then Peter, filled with the Holy Spirit, said to them, "Rulers of the people and elders, if we are being examined today concerning a good deed done to a cripple, by what means this man has been healed, be it known to you all, and to all the people of Israel, that by the the name of Jesus Christ of Nazareth, whom you crucified, whom God raised from the dead, by Him this man is standing before you well. This is the Stone which was rejected by you builders, but which has become the Head of the corner. And there is salvation is no one else, for there is no other name under heaven given among men by which we must be saved."

Acts 4:1-12

POWER
Before Men

One of the great heroes in the history of the missions of the church is Ramón Lull, a Majorcan of noble birth, who was to become the founder of the first mission seminary. Like other great figures in the church such as Francis of Assisi and St. Augustine, Lull in his youth led a profligate life made easy by the great wealth at his disposal. The sudden change in his life that brought him to the church completely altered his life. We are not sure of the incident that provoked the change. Some say he had a vision of the Christ. Others say that a shocking incident in one of his escapades forced him to go for spiritual help. However, what prompted his conversion is not our chief interest in him. What is significant about his work is the fact that he undertook an extremely difficult mission. He was educated in theology, philosophy, and the languages. He founded a mission school, and then he himself took to the field to witness to Christ among the Moslems. In north Africa he dressed like a Moslem and worked among the people. Whenever he gained a following, he was sure to be persecuted and ill-treated. Finally he was rescued from his last beating by some Genoese sailors who carried him aboard ship and sailed for his homeland, but he died just before they came to Majorca. His story impresses us with the fact that he had power before men.

Lull's story and those like it are reminiscent of the first reports of the missionary activity of the disciples in Jerusalem. In the holy city Peter and John used the incident of a healing at the temple to make a bold testimony to our Lord Jesus. We have that testimony before us. What is striking about the incident is that we can see that the disciples are changed men. That was already true of the disciples at Pentecost. Earlier, while the disciples were following Jesus through His ministry, they likewise could rise on occasion to great confession, only to vacillate. Now, however, their boldness had a great consistency to it, and they were men who displayed maturity in the Spirit. They were not likely to be threatened by those things that bothered them before. They were not afraid of the enemies of Jesus. They were men who knew what must be done, and they were willing to do it whatever the cost might be. As with the heroes that were to follow after them, we cannot always psychologize their motives and the degree of change in their lives. In common they had the gift of the Spirit. What does it mean to have the gift of the Spirit?

To have the gift of the Spirit involves a clear testimony to the life, death, and resurrection of Jesus Christ. What is important about that is to note that such power is available to us all who know and confess Jesus Christ. The gifts that God distributed here were not limited to some man who had an extraordinary gift of the Spirit. Peter and John preached straight Gospel. This was power, and it was an annoyance to the religious leaders. They were annoyed because Peter and John "were teaching the people and proclaiming in Jesus the resurrection from the dead." There are those who believe that the issue here was more political than it was religious. Somehow the two are not always easily divided. It is interesting to note that the leaders who protested this preaching of the resurrection were the Sadducees, who did not believe in the doctrine of the resurrection. Whether they were exercised about this preaching incident because they thought it might substantiate the teaching of their enemies, the Pharisees, is hard to say. Did they think of this teaching and preaching as a direct threat to their position? Or was it that they were upset because Peter and John had caused such a great commotion? Were Peter and John disturbing the peace as well as their opponents' own version of orthodoxy? The adversaries felt something about this occasion that made them uneasy. They were threatened by the possibility that this preaching might bring a catastrophe to their lives.

We should note this well. The preaching of the Gospel is the preaching of a revolutionary message. It is the preaching of the change which God brings into the lives of men. We may expect that when the Gospel is truly preached that there are many who will feel severely threatened. Not everyone accepts or believes our Gospel. Many resist. But even in their resistance they may be greatly disturbed by it. I can recall from one of the first years of my ministry that I was invited to call on a man dying of cancer. After several visits he began to show hostile reaction to the Gospel because it contradicted his reason. His wife finally asked me to visit no more, because he was greatly disturbed after each visit. Whether he finally surrendered to the Gospel of forgiveness and reconciliation in Christ, the Risen One, we will not know until eternity. But this reaction of disturbance is not uncommon. Yet because people are disturbed does not mean that they will believe. No matter how hard we try, no matter how much we may preach or teach, there are those who will resist the good gift of God's love in Christ even though they may be disturbed by the news that Christ was crucified but is risen from the dead.

What is there about this Gospel of the death and resurrection of Jesus Christ for the reconciliation of the world that creates disturbance? We know that this Gospel is the proclamation of the high price that God was willing to pay for the saving of mankind. God was prompted to die for us. This Gospel also places a high evaluation on man in that it testifies that God was and is willing to give to man the blessing of eternity. All of this is disturbing to men who, like the rulers in Jerusalem, want to use the state or any power to run roughshod over men or to use them simply as the pawns of the state. The Word of God with its honest appraisal of man, on the one hand, and its gracious promise of redemption on the other, is disturbing to anyone who wants to exploit man. The Christian Gospel is heresy to all totalitarianism, to all exploitation of the poor, to all injustice, to all race oppression. The Christian Gospel with its sacrificial love for men is also heresy to the economic reactionaries who exploit the creation and man. The Christian Gospel with its emphasis upon reconciliation and forgiveness is also heresy to the rightists and the leftists who insist on their way as the only way. If the Christian Gospel is heresy today to authorities somewhere behind the iron curtain or the bamboo curtain, you can be sure that it is that also to some in New York, or Atlanta, or Indianapolis.

Clarence Jordan has rendered a free translation of portions of the New Testament which are called his "cotton patch version." Jordan seeks to translate and paraphrase the New Testament in such a way that modern man will not only catch the bite of the Scriptures but will also be able to apply them to his own situation. In his cotton-patch version of Acts he translates that the authorities "were plenty mad" at Peter and John. Maybe that is something that people will understand about the reaction that set in. But this also gives us something to think about. We ought to wonder if we are really sharing the Gospel of the death and resurrection of our Lord if we get no reaction from others. Is the failure in the church today due to the apathy of the world or to apathy in the church? If the world is not turned on because of our Gospel, then may we expect it to turn against us? At Jerusalem the church experienced both reactions. Have we today turned the world off because we have no convictions about this Gospel, because we believe that it has no power, because we believe that it has no applications to the lives of men? When have we last caused a commotion in the lives of our neighbors because we preached this Jesus Christ to someone or shared the goodness of His love with someone?

Ultimately we must hope that, however people would react to our Gospel, they will ask the kind of question that was put to Peter and John, "By what power or by what name did you do this?" No matter how great or how many the gifts were among the apostles, they had no greater gift than to force men to involuntarily ask the question, "By what power or by what name did you do this?" When we have that power to make the world stop short and ask us what it is that we are doing, then we can be sure that we are in the tradition of the apostles.

Apart from what outsiders may say or not say, we are forced to ask questions of ourselves. How are we doing? Have we been performing of late in such a way that men have to stop and ask us where it is we get the resources for doing great things? Has there been anything about our lives that has forced men to stop in wonder and amazement to check out our credentials? Or do we just blend with the wallpaper? Are we like the fellow who was being introduced by his host? As the host went around the room introducing the guests he said something about each. When he came to our friend, he said simply, "And this is John Doe. He doesn't do anything. He just is." Is that how we must think of the church today? It doesn't do anything? It just is? The question is an important one. There are many who contend that the church has no power, no authority, today. It just is, and the sooner they get rid of it the better.

Yet the question for us is a wrong one. We are not going to stir up power and strength, vigor and vitality for addressing our Gospel to the world by asking ourselves, "How are we doing?" We have the answer to that. We are doing poorly. We have always done poorly, and we will never do well enough. But we are not going to get hung up on that point. It is the very nature of the Gospel we share to proclaim forgiveness even for this failure of not doing well enough. But our Gospel is so radical in its grace that we are propelled and compelled by it to go out again and again to share this good news of God's love for all men. It is a remarkable fact that nowhere do we hear Peter mulling over his past denial of our Lord. But we hear him preaching with great hope and vigor the Gospel that forgave him. So also Paul mentions that though he had been the most radical persecutor of the church, he was now determined to know nothing but Jesus Christ and Him crucified. We too can rebound from any failures we have had in sharing this Gospel, any timidity or fear, and become immersed in this power which God freely gives us to make us bold with His power before men.

power *to Die*

Now when they heard these things they were enraged, and they ground their teeth against him. But he, full of the Holy Spirit, gazed into heaven and saw the glory of God, and Jesus standing at the right hand of God; and he said, "Behold, I see the heavens opened, and the Son of Man standing at the right hand of God." But they cried out with a loud voice and stopped their ears and rushed together upon him. Then they cast him out of the city and stoned him; and the witnesses laid down their garments at the feet of a young man named Saul. And as they were stoning Stephen, he prayed, "Lord Jesus, receive my spirit." And he knelt down and cried with a loud voice, "Lord, do not hold this sin against them." And when he had said this, he fell asleep.

Acts 7:54-60

POWER to Die

Taylor Caldwell's novel *Testimony of Two Men* is the story of a terribly complex young medic of the turn of the 20th century who is impatient with the slowness with which his colleagues adopt the new discoveries of medicine. Dr. Jonathan Ferrier possesses integrity to a fault. He is unable to compromise with the prejudices, dishonesty, and failures of the society around him. He makes more enemies than friends as he serves his community with impeccable faithfulness to his profession. As his community shows him more and more ingratitude and ruthlessness, he senses less and less the value of living. Yet as a doctor he places a premium on life and on the need to prolong life. With expert care he helps many to live, but he keeps asking himself the question, "Why? Why should anyone want to live in a world that can be and is as cruel as the world of man?" His despondency is the desperate cry of the suicide who asks the questions and answers it by taking his own life. Jonathan often asked himself why he should try to keep the suicidal person from taking his life. At one point he believes that the person who commits suicide has more courage than the person who lives. But that is a good question. Does the suicidal person have courage? Or is he copping out and quitting because he has absolutely no courage left whatsoever? Or is it that he is so convinced that he does not have to meet a Maker or Creator that he can challenge life with his death? Really, does not the courage to live really come when we have the power to die in quite another spirit?

Some of this may sound as fanciful theory or argument, but in reality it is not. It is important for us to recognize that much of our fear in life is related to our fear of death. And it is important to see that great courage to live or die comes when we have the power to die. We are not to suggest that the Christian should not want to live. Nor are we promoting an otherworldly concept of the world in which the Christian becomes dulled to the problems of this world. Far from it, we are talking about the kind of bravery and heroics that enables people to face up to the problems of life because they have the power to die. That is to say: Those people who can afford to be courageous in life are those who are prepared and willing to die. Christians can manifest a kind of holy recklessness because they know that their lives have been redeemed by the God who created them and loved them with an eternal love. That kind of talk does not gain a great deal of sympathy in the world because people entertain the assumption that we cheapen life or downgrade it when we do not make this life and this world the most, or the more, important.

This objection is neither fruitful nor valid because, on the one hand, life measured against the long haul of history is too brief for anyone to seriously entertain the notion that it—physical life in this creation, this world, and this history—is the whole story of man. On the other hand, the Christian responds that this life is the gift of God. It is precious for that reason alone. But it is also the life in this world, in this history that God has redeemed with the precious blood of His Son Jesus Christ, and it is this life which God will raise to eternity. As Christians we have a picture of the continuity of life in the hands of God. As Christians we have a large view of life. We can risk life in holy causes because in the hands of God we know that all the risk has been taken out of life. This is what we learn from the story of Stephen the Martyr. In the Book of Acts the story is a very prominent one and is certainly meant to teach us the importance of the faith confessed in the early church. Stephen was one of seven who had been chosen by the congregation at Jerusalem to serve in a kind of diaconate to care for the needs of the poor. However, it appears that these men not only cared for the daily distribution but that they also were capable of witnessing to the Lord Jesus Christ. Stephen is an example of those who are prepared to witness and to die for the witness that they make to the Lord Jesus Christ.

Before we examine carefully the person and character of Stephen as we know him from this story, it is worth looking at the enemies of Stephen. These were people who were chagrined because they failed in a disputation with Stephen. They thought that Stephen had misinterpreted Moses and the Prophets. They could not stand up to his testimony, so they brought false charges against him and accused him of blasphemy against the Law and the Prophets. In his own defense before the council, as Luke records, Stephen gave a long testimony, which is really a fresh interpretation of the history of Israel from Abraham to David in the light of Israel's refusal to accept God's revelation through His prophets. Stephen then made the point that, as Israel before them had rejected the prophets, so now Jerusalem had rejected the Lord Jesus Christ. The enemies had closed their minds and hearts to the message of Jesus. They had refused His great and mighty acts as signs of His Messiahship. They had refused the word of the apostles. And even now they were refusing the word of the deacon Stephen. They had not done so on valid grounds—not on the basis of sound and good reasoning. Their refusal had been based on purely emotional grounds. All the while they tried to portray themselves as maintaining a position of orthodoxy and loyalty to the Law. However, their emotional reaction kept them from hearing the real Word of God in Christ Jesus.

Luke records that the reaction of enemies was typical: "Now when they heard these things they were enraged, and they ground their teeth against him." The description is one of emotions run amuck. Not only do the people fail to have an open mind and heart to the message of Stephen, but now they also lose full control of their emotions and become enraged. In animal-like fashion they now grind their teeth against him. Like dogs snarling at him they show the fierceness of their anger and their need and desire to attack him. Actually they have already lost control of their minds. They lost rationality, and instead of exercising good and sound reason they surrender to emotional fury, snarling and howling. Their conduct becomes savage. They are now the primitive hunters and Stephen is the hunted one. They must give vent to their fury. When Stephen in perfect composure gains a vision of the heavens opened, they are even more enraged, and they "cried with a loud voice and stopped their ears and rushed together upon him" (7:57). Anger, impatience, and hatred conspire in the hearts of these men to make them stop their ears. No longer do they only refuse to believe what Stephen said. Now they also refuse to hear. They cease to think above the ears and resort to physical action. Directed by prejudice and self-interest, they rush at Stephen full force.

They turn to throw stones. Somehow they presume they had the greater force. Their first presumption is that they know more than Stephen. Their second is that they do not need the word of Stephen. Their third presumption is that they can overpower him with the force of physical power. That is a common notion in the world. People believe that they can gain their point by some show of power.

It is a common assumption in our time that the world of

physical science or any material force is far superior to the world of spirit and love. But what should really shock us about this story is that the enemies in this setting are religious men. As religious leaders they oppose the Gospel of the Lord Jesus Christ in the name of Holy Scripture, of Moses and the Prophets. We should remember that these are the men who laid claim to orthodoxy and conservativism. But what we should remember above all is that they were provoked to anger by the proclamation of the Gospel. From this we should learn not to be one bit surprised that when the Gospel is preached, it stirs up all kinds of animosity and trouble. We should learn that we can expect the enemies of the Gospel to become loud and vehement in their denouncement of the preachers of the Gospel. We can expect them to resort to all kinds of threats, to acts of force and power.

On the other hand, we learn something very comforting from the story of Stephen. We said that this man was a man who was prepared to die. He was prepared for the death of a martyr because of the kind of confession he made. His strength for this awful hour was not his own. He gained this strength from the very One whom he confessed. As he confessed the Lord Jesus Christ he was one with Him who was his Savior. He knew and was assured that the One who had died for him would not permit him to die alone. He knew that the One who had gone to the grave before him had also blazed a way to eternity through the tomb for him. He knew that the One whom he confessed was also the One who would confess him before His Father in heaven. He knew also that the One whom he confessed was the One who had forgiven whatever sins he had committed, whatever he had done to grieve his God, whatever he had failed to do under the Law. He believed the Gospel which said that Jesus was His Savior, His Lord, His Christ. His very confession to the men who jeered him was that the Law had been fulfilled for them by the Lord Jesus Christ. This is what he was pointing to. But they were still defending their own righteousness by the terms of the Law as they understood it. They had to be violent against him because his message judged them as at the same time it offered the saving Gospel to them.

With this powerful faith in his mind and heart Stephen was prepared for the worst that these men could do to him, because he knew that God had already done His best for him. They could try to take his life, but he knew that God had already given him a life that cannot be taken away. With this kind of conviction he could employ the gift of prayer that his Savior had bestowed on him. He could pray as the Lord Jesus had taught him to pray. He had the power to die peacefully because he also had the power to pray. Just as our Lord had prayed to the Father from the cross, so under the hail of stones he prays to our Lord, "Lord Jesus, receive my spirit." Then also in the spirit of Christ he prays, "Lord, do not hold this sin against them." There was power to die. When we have the power to forgive we have the power to face the worst kind of attack the enemies can make on us. No matter what their plans are, we know that the cause of the Gospel will not permit us to engage in their kind of tactics or their violent kind of rage. The cause of our offense to them is the Gospel for which we are ready to die. And we win. They lose when they think they win. There was one present there who learned that lesson. The scene remained indelibly impressed upon his soul, and it was only a short time later that the scene came to haunt Saul on the road to Damascus.

power

for Interpretation

But an angel of the Lord said to Philip, "Rise and go toward the south to the road that goes down from Jerusalem to Gaza." This is a desert road. And he rose and went. And behold, an Ethiopian, a eunuch, a minister of Candace, the queen of the Ethiopians, in charge of all her treasure, had come to Jerusalem to worship and was returning; seated in his chariot, he was reading the prophet Isaiah.

Acts 8:26-28

POWER
for Interpretation

In our story, when the apostle Philip asks the Ethiopian eunuch the question, "Do you understand what you are reading?" the eunuch answers, "How can I, unless someone guides me?" The question of the Ethiopian poses a great problem in our approach to Scripture and its interpretation. Protestants in the past have given a great deal of lip service to the principle that Scriptures are so understandable that one could come to faith on his own when left to the reading of Scripture by himself. However, when we search for examples of this principle we find few illustrations. Our own experience makes us question that notion, for often our people confess that they are confused when reading Scripture on their own. On top of that, we have this story, in which the novice with Scripture begs the interpreter for help. The Roman Church, on the other hand, has had a very rigid position which demands that Scripture cannot be interpreted apart from the teaching office of the church, which is highly dependent upon tradition. Now we realize the flaws that exist in the Protestant principles, and the Church of Rome has also greatly modified the flaws in its position. The answer, of course, lies in the question of the Ethiopian, "How can I [understand] unless someone guides me [in the reading of Scripture]?" While we cannot on the basis of this story elaborate in detail the basic rules that do help in the interpretation of Scripture, we can find a few helps that give us power for interpretation.

The Ethiopian explained to Philip where he was in the reading of Scripture. He was reading the beautiful Suffering Servant chapter from Isaiah (53). Luke goes on: "Then Philip opened his mouth, and beginning with this Scripture he told him the Good News." Very simply and with sympathy Philip began where every good teacher should begin. He started teaching the man at the point where he was. The sharing that Philip had to do was in keeping with the experience of the man. He did not refer the Ethiopian to something that was remote and had no bearing on his ability to understand. A good educational principle is that we move in on those experiences which, people find, beg for an answer from the living Word which our God has given us. What failures we will be with the Good News if we are trying to answer the kind of questions people are neither asking or want answered! When we fail to tie our presentation of the Good News into the living and real experiences of the people, the news will not be good news, but only so much more information which people may or may not find interesting. If the Good News is only so much fact that the people file away with the family album it will be of no value to them.

The temptation for us who are the bearers of the Good News is to think that if we teach anything at all, then we are doing our jobs. There is a teaching task to be done, to be sure. Jesus gave the command "to teach all nations." But this teaching task is more than feeding information. This is not something that can be handled by a teaching machine or a computer. This teaching is a discipline, that is, it makes disciples of men. This teaching is bound up with the power of the Spirit, who has the power to change men by what He brings into their minds and hearts. This teaching is the work of God, for it is God who is our Teacher as we handle the Word He has given us through His Spirit.

It is the very same Word by which God fashioned man and made him what he was. When by the Word God created man, He also sought to lead and guide him, to teach him. When man turned aside from that divine teaching, then God called him to account by His Word. He said, "Adam, where are you?" That is beginning where man is. That is where we must always begin. If we are to call man to account because he hides in the garden of his sin, then we must use the Word of the Law for that purpose. If, on the other hand, he lives in the terror of his sin, then we must come to him with that Word from God which would lead him to an apprehension of the mercies of God. If he lives in utter confusion, then we must use that Word of God which would lead him out of his darkness.

God does have a Word for us in our time. We can begin with man wherever he is. The art of interpretation, however, will depend upon the circumstances in which we find man. We make a mistake if we think that we can bend this Word to our own will. We are to interpret it in such a way that it speaks God's will to man. We cannot use this Word for our own purposes to make it back up our wishes, our desires, our ideas, our ambitions. When we interpret this Word, we must let it be what it is: the Word of God to man. Man distorts the Word when he fails to let it speak what God intends that it should speak. There have been many abuses, with men handling the Word to suit their fancy. We must begin with the assumption that this is God's Word, that He addresses it to us to do something with us. We begin where man is, but we don't stop there, for the purpose of the Word is to bring man to understand where God is in his life. All of the Bible classes, the Bible series, the Bible quizzes, and whatever learning there may be of the Bible – these are of no avail unless we permit each confrontation with the Word to be a confrontation with his holy God who would speak to man. Interpretation begins here. We must begin with the fact that God's Word is the means by which He would have a word with us.

From our story we learn a second clue for interpretation that should be of great value to us. When the Ethiopian and Philip discussed the Isaiah passage which they read together, the Ethiopian asked Philip of whom the prophet was writing. "Then Philip opened his mouth, and beginning with this Scripture, he told him of the Good News of Jesus." Philip saw that the great Messianic figure of Isaiah's prophecy was our Lord Jesus Christ. He undoubtedly related how he saw that Jesus in His life, death, and resurrection was the One who was the fulfillment of all that the prophets had preached. For us it should also be so. The whole purpose of our interpretation should be to lead people to the Lord Jesus Christ. Luther was that great interpreter of Scripture who knew the Scripture so well and moved so freely in it. His ability to interpret the Psalms and all of the Old Testament in the light of the work of Jesus Christ is amazing. He had the basic conviction that the Scriptures are to bring us the message of salvation in Jesus Christ. He held that this was their sole purpose. Scripture exists for no other reason. He was learned and well read enough to know that there is other beautiful literature in the world, some of it surpassing many parts of Scripture in beauty. But all of the great literature in the world could do nothing for our salvation. The Scriptures, he said, are the cradle of Christ. The key to the Word of God is *was Christum treibet,* that is, "which bears Christ."

If we are to be true interpreters of the Word we must hold to this same view and be as radical as Dr. Martin Luther was. Luther had good precedents for his view. Our Lord Himself confronted those great teachers in Israel who were far better schooled in the Word of God, the Scriptures, than were His disciples. He accused them of searching the Scriptures—and searching for eternal life—yet missing the very heart of Scripture which was He Himself. And He told them, "If you believed Moses you would believe Me, for he wrote of Me" (John 5:46). Debate and argument, dialog and discussion about the Scriptures are empty and meaningless unless we see clearly that our whole purpose is to lead men to a clear understanding of the Messiahship and the Lordship of Jesus. Much breath and argument is being wasted today by those who uphold a certain interpretation of Scripture which they think is true and right, but which shows little regard for helping men to see Jesus as their Savior. And this I can say plainly and clearly to every layman: he can determine whether an argument is valid or not by asking if it leads or does not lead men to see Jesus Christ as their Savior. The second clue is as clear as we can make it: Power for interpretation must center in the Lord Jesus Christ.

The third clue for interpretation is that interpretation must also include application. If the Word of God grabs man where he is and leads him to the Lord Jesus Christ, it also calls for action. The Ethiopian in our story commanded his chariot driver to stop that he might be baptized. The Word that had caught him was no speculation or simply an idea. The application fitted to his own life. The Word of God had come into his life and literally had called it to a halt. The old way of moving on had been brought to a stop. There was a new way for him, and he was to be a part of it, because God was now the Mover in his life. To interpret the Word, we must always ask how this Word is to be applied to us and what action is expected of us. Luther rescued Biblical interpretation from the very complicated and dry art that it had become in the medieval church. The Word then was interpreted in many ways which permitted men to dodge its great import for their lives. Luther would always ask: How are you applying the Word to yourself? What action does it require of you? How will you apply any Scripture? If you simply apply some ethical or moral teaching requiring some proper action on your part, that would be missing the point also. Then you may as well read *Aesop's Fables* or *Poor Richard's Almanac.* You see, already you are learning how to be an interpreter.

To have power for interpretation we do not use the clues one at a time or in isolation. We have to keep all of them in mind at all times. If we begin with the fact that the Word comes to man where he is, and that the purpose of the Word is to lead him to Christ, then the action to which it leads him will also be in Christ Jesus. In the story the application is very neat and simple. The Ethiopian was led to be baptized. Tradition has it that the Coptic church which later existed in Ethiopia stemmed from his conversion. But what is the benefit of the story for us? For all of us Luke has clearly intended that we should take heart from the story and learn how it is that the Holy Spirit works in the lives of people and continues His work on earth. This is how God builds His church, how He adds people through the application of the Word in their lives. For us that should give great comfort. But it should also prompt action in us. For if we are comforted by this Word, we should also see that the power of interpretation belongs to us. We can use this Word. We can use it together. We can use it for one another when we see that it is His Word and that, when we keep it to the purposes for which He has given it, He will bless our interpretation and use it for a blessing to others.

power *for Witness*

Now the apostles and the brethren who were in Judea heard that the Gentiles also had received the Word of God. So when Peter went up to Jerusalem, the circumcision party criticized him, saying, "Why did you go to uncircumcised men and eat with them?" But Peter began and explained to them in order: "I was in the city of Joppa praying; and in a trance I saw a vision, something descending, like a great sheet, let down from heaven by four corners; and it came down to me. Looking at it closely I observed animals and beasts of prey and reptiles and birds of the air. And I heard a voice saying to me, 'Rise, Peter; kill and eat.' But I said, 'No, Lord; for nothing common or unclean has ever entered my mouth.' But the voice answered a second time from heaven, 'What God has cleansed you must not call common.' This happened three times, and all was drawn up again into heaven. At that very moment three men arrived at the house in which we were, sent to me from Caesarea. And the Spirit told me to go with them, making no distinction. These six brethren also accompanied me, and we entered the man's house. And he told us how he had seen the angel standing in his house and saying, 'Send to Joppa and bring Simon called Peter; he will declare to you a message by which you will be saved, you and all your household. As I began to speak, the Holy Spirit fell on them just as on us at the beginning. And I remembered the Word of the Lord, how he said, 'John baptized with water, but you shall be baptized with the Holy Spirit.' If then God gave the same gift to them as He gave to us when we believed in the Lord Jesus Christ, who was I that I could withstand God?" When they heard this they were silenced. And they glorified God, saying, "Then to the Gentiles also God has granted repentance unto life."

Acts 11:1-18

POWER for Witness

The religious movement in this country was highly dependent on the Methodist circuit rider who moved faithfully on the frontiers of the nation to carry the Gospel of Jesus Christ to the people. The more orthodox and traditional denominations moved slowly in the cities and almost entirely devoted their energies to caring for immigrant groups of their own nationality and confessional persuasion. The Methodist circuit riders, on the other hand, worked tirelessly in the effort to push the Gospel out into the bush and into every area of life in which people were unattended by the ministry. The Methodists had their origin in the early 18th century in a club at Oxford University. Because the small group of students who comprised the club went about their Biblical study, church attendance, and Christian service with great faithfulness and orderliness, they were derisively called "Methodists." Brothers John and Charles Wesley became leaders of the group which later blossomed into the Methodist movement and the Methodist Church. Early the Wesleys visited prisons to minister to debtors and thieves, started a school for children in poverty, rode on horseback to preach to the poor in the country, and started a similar movement of preaching and service in America. What triggered this great religious movement was the sympathy that the Wesleys had for the poor and those neglected by the churches. They discovered that the Gospel was meant for these economic and spiritual outcasts. When they discovered this, they discovered the power for witness.

One would think that it should be perfectly obvious that

we must preach the Gospel to all creatures. That should be obvious because that is what our Lord commanded. We give lip service to this mission over and over again. We put it into our mission literature and make the appeal repeatedly. There is hardly anyone in our congregations who would not insist that we must take seriously the command of our Lord. Yet when we go to put this matter into practice and do that which our Lord has commanded, we see how quickly our people limit the command of our Lord. Then all kinds of members are willing to put restrictions on who it is that we can serve with the Gospel of Jesus Christ. There are those members who do not want the money for missions to go overseas. There are some who think that the overseas mission must be limited to people in Western free nations and that no money should be spent for missions or relief in communist nations. There are some who do not want to share the Gospel with the poor. Some do not want us to work in the black community. Others would not have us share the Gospel with those whom they regard as immoral, those who have been freed from prison, or those whose lives have been tainted in any way.

The business then of sharing the Gospel of Jesus Christ some people would limit to those who they feel are deserving or worthy of the Gospel. Such attitudes are to be roundly and soundly condemned, because they limit and hurt the very work of God. We know from the very kind of story which we have before us that such attitudes are wrong. Israel had come to believe that the covenant promises of God were to be limited to those who were born to the families of Israel. All of that was in contrast to the universal character of the promises of grace which God gave to ancient Israel. Much of ancient Israel's life was shaped by the concept of universal grace and mercy for the world. The perversion of these teachings was obvious in Israel's history from time to time. However, the greatest perversion of this teaching came after the return from the Babylonian Captivity, when the children of Israel tried to assure themselves that this would never happen again. They became exclusive, restricting all religious practices to themselves. They greatly limited their proselyting activity; they became very rigid in their membership practices. This was no small problem then for the apostles, who wondered if the work of our Lord Jesus Christ had the same limitations as those which they knew from the practice of the faith in the Old Covenant. It was this concern that was answered by the story before us.

Peter had gone to the home of a centurion, Cornelius, sharing the Gospel and eating with him in his home. The leaders of the judaizing faction of the church of Jerusalem were offended because Peter had extended the blessings of the Gospel to Gentiles. This was a disturbing new idea that was sure to break down the Jewish character of the Gospel. Peter then related that he had had a vision in which God had told him that he could eat of the animals which had been declared "unclean" under the Old Covenant. He learned from the vision that he should no longer consider Gentiles as unclean nor exclude them from the application of the Gospel. Peter said to them who were jealous of his action, "If then God gave the same gift to them as He gave to us when we believed in the Lord Jesus Christ, who was I that I could withstand God?" Must we not all learn how to say these words? Who are we to limit the work of God, the operation of His Spirit, the boundaries of His work? It is He who has redeemed and cleansed the world of all its sin by the precious blood of His Son. It is He who is able to give and who desires to give the power of His Holy Spirit to men so that they may believe. Who are we that we could withstand God in His generous efforts to save the world?

After Peter had related his story and had given his interpretation of it, the Judaizers "were silenced," Luke writes, adding that "they glorified God saying, 'Then to the Gentiles also God has granted repentance unto life.' " The light dawned on these people that God was not only capable of saving others but that He was also perfectly willing to do so. It was supposedly a great moment for them when they came to this realization. Luke mentions it, of course, because it is the very intention of his Gospel and his Book of Acts to make it clear to the Gentile world that the Gospel of Jesus Christ is intended for them. So, of course, when we read this story in that context we realize the importance of this narrative. However, when we think about it a little while we realize how presumptuous it is for people to want to restrict the Gospel. It is presumptuous, because it is only by the sheer grace of God that anyone is saved—including us. Why should we think that it is harder for God to save someone other than we? Why should we think that our coming to faith was more natural than someone else's? Why should we think that somehow we are better qualified to become the children of God than someone else? If we entertain these ideas in any way, then we have not come to a proper understanding of how it is that a man is saved. For from the Law we learn that all men are sinners. From the Law we discover the depth of our sin and the fact that we should die for our sin. But from the Gospel we learn that we have a gracious God who gave His Son into death for our sakes.

Our own salvation depends on the very fact that God has made it possible for all men to come to faith and the knowledge of the truth. When we exclude the possibility of any man being saved by God's mercy, then we jeopardize and put into doubt the question of whether God can save *us*. Our salvation by God's grace is dependent on the universal character of God's love. We had better all understand that and understand it clearly. It is difficult for us at times to remember and to accept this. Some suggest that these Judaizers quickly forgot the lesson Peter taught them and in a short time harassed the church with their indignant attitude. Whether Paul was to suffer from these very people, we do not know, but we do know that Paul had to contend vigorously with Judaizers later. Even Peter seems to have weakened in his position later, and Paul had to call him to account for the matter. What this says to us is that we must guard against this kind of presumptuousness all the time. Our pride is so natural and so pervasive that we must war against it at all times lest it stand in the way of the preaching of the Gospel to all men.

When, however, we are aware of what it is that God has done for the whole world in His Son Jesus Christ, then we are given a new perspective of our situation and the condition of the world. Despite the bad turn of events due to man's sin, the Gospel of our Lord Jesus Christ tells us that God is able to create life out of death, to cover sin with Christ's holiness, to turn despair into joy, and fear into hope. We discover through the Gospel that God does not want us to live in alienation and polarization but that He wants to bring us all into the unity of the Gospel. We learn then that, instead of being reluctant to see the Gospel shared with men, we have reason to be full of joy and to be eager to share the blessings of the Gospel. We do not have to look to ourselves to decide who shall and who shall not hear our Gospel. We do not have to look to ourselves to find the power to witness to this Gospel. We do not have to look to ourselves to find some way in which we can make this Gospel effective. The power for witnessing is found in the Gospel itself. We do not have to manipulate or manage it in any special way. That is of great comfort for us, because that takes the kind of burden off us that seems to bother us the most. We do not have to worry whether we are good enough witnesses, whether we have said everything right, and whether our witness will be effective. The Gospel tells us that God wants it preached to all people. The Gospel also gives the power by which we can be witnesses.

We have mentioned John and Charles Wesley as founders of the Methodist Church. There were others, of course. When America called for someone to come as a circuit rider and to do here what the Wesleys had done in England, a young Englishman by the name of Francis Asbury stepped forward. He took up the work in America with great zeal and determination. He visited practically every state in the Union of his day. He was called the "Man Without a Home." He received little for his tireless efforts. He endured great hardships. But he did not mind. He gloried in His work, which he considered to be the effort to turn the world upside down for the sake of the Gospel. He was a great spirit in the history of the mission of the church in America. If we are to recover his zeal, then we need only be convinced and believe that we must follow the directives which are inherent in this story. We believe that God has redeemed the world. We believe that God has given power for repentance. And God also gives us the power for witness through the joy which He gives to us.

power amid Chaos

Now after these events Paul resolved in the Spirit to pass through Macedonia and Achaia and go to Jerusalem, saying, "After I have been there, I must also see Rome." And having sent into Macedonia two of his helpers, Timothy and Erastus, he himself stayed in Asia for a while.

About that time there arose no little stir concerning the Way. For a man named Demetrius, a silversmith, who made silver shrines of Artemis, brought no little business to the craftsmen. These he gathered together, with the workmen of like occupation and said, "Men, you know that from this business we have our wealth. And you see and hear that not only at Ephesus, but almost throughout all Asia this Paul has persuaded and turned away a considerable company of people, saying that gods made with hands are not gods. And there is danger not only that this trade of ours may come into disrepute but also that the temple of the great goddess Artemis may count for nothing, and that she may even be deposed from her magnificence, she whom all Asia and the world worship."

Acts 19:21-27

POWER amid Chaos

Jeffrey K. Hadden, a sociologist, has written a book called *The Gathering Storm in the Churches.* Dr. Hadden sees a growing gap developing between clergymen and laymen. This he asserts is the crisis which threatens the Christian church in the next century. He indicates that the crisis is so deep and so severe that one has to question seriously the importance and influence of the Christian church for some time to come. Basically, the author observes, the difference between the clergy and laity is really on the role of the church. The clergy are more apt to emphasize the prophetic role of the church and its need to face up to the challenges of society. The laity, on the other hand, are more inclined to look to the church for comfort and support in their own roles. The question is, How can the church come to grips with the modern world that has become so secular and so highly materialistic? Whether we are familiar with this kind of formal study or not, all of us have been exposed in some way to the current arguments in general Protestantism about the role of the church. Much of the flap that has developed on the larger scene of Protestantism and also in Roman Catholicism has caused a great deal of unsettledness. There are charges and suspicions about doctrine, purpose, and authority everywhere. For this reason we should look carefully at the story before us to learn something of how, in this kind of crisis, we may have power amid chaos.

The story before us gives a rather vivid picture of a riot at the city of Ephesus. The people were rioting in response to the presence of the apostle Paul. Paul had been working in the city for some time, and considerable success attended his evangelistic effort. The Lord had used Paul for effecting much good and for winning many hearts for the cause of the Gospel. However, while Paul was still there and making plans to go back to Jerusalem, a silversmith by the name of Demetrius stirred up the people against Paul. Not only his business of fashioning idols but also the other industries that supplied him with materials were hurt by Paul's preaching to rescue the people from idolatry. Paul had caused a deep depression in the idol business. You can guess what followed. Demetrius incited the people to riot. They dragged the colleagues of Paul into the theater and wanted to do something to them. As usual, the mob was mindless, some of the people not even knowing why they were there. For two hours the people screamed, "Great is Artemis of the Ephesians!" The people had been worked up into this frenzy over the economics of the situation. What was bad for business was bad for the people. There was no appreciation of the liberty and freedom Paul brought by his gospel. There was no willingness to examine the changes Paul encouraged through what he preached. There was no attention to the message. The people reacted emotionally because they felt that the institution they cherished was threatened.

There is a lesson here for us. We hear of the kind of reactions to changes that might be instituted in the church or in the society by teachers or preachers of the Gospel. As for our own reactions, we had better be sure that we are not reacting purely on the basis of emotion. It is not wise for us to react negatively simply because we think that to pursue the implications of the Gospel is going to cost us something. How unfaithful we would be to our Lord if we failed to listen to the message of the Gospel because it would be bad for business! And yet this is what some people are saying. We all have heard people say that we cannot do something in the church because it would offend someone and they might stop giving to the church treasury. There are many today who suggest that the troubles in the church are the direct cause of the financial squeeze the church is suffering. All of this overlooks our obligation to accept willingly the losses and hardships that the Gospel inflicts on us. We should learn not to be dissuaded by the pocketbook when the Spirit of God makes some demands on us.

The results at Ephesus hold also some comfort for us. The threatening and terrifying scene which Luke pictures for us is no different from the kind of disturbances that we have become so accustomed to reading and hearing about in our times. Paul had not been dragged into the theater, but he considered going to the rescue of his friends there to make some kind of speech to satisfy the crowd. Cooler heads prevailed. Some of his friends who were a part of the government understood the temper of the crowd better than he. They kept Paul from going. It was the town clerk who arose in the theater to make the speech which calmed the situation. He argued with the people that Paul and his team of evangelists had done no harm to the community, and if Demetrius and the craftsmen had a legitimate complaint, they could be heard in the courts. With that the crowd was dismissed and peace prevailed. Paul and his colleagues were safe. They had experienced the intervention of God once more. They were saved by God's providence in an unexpected way. They found friends and defenders where they would not have expected them, and civil law was the means by which they were ultimately delivered. Here Paul could not resort to some Gospel message to save the day, because quite obviously he could get no hearing from people who were so hostile to God's cause. Yet God used civil servants as His agents for the protection of His cause and for opening the door to the Gospel He wanted preached.

We have something to learn here also. We make a serious error if we believe we can conquer the hearts of all men with the Gospel of Jesus Christ. There are times when hostility to that message is so great that we can expect that people will not even listen to us. We can expect that the world will demonstrate against the Gospel when it is sure that the Gospel will endanger its systems and way of life. Then God must rule the emotions and passions of men in another way. We then pray that God would somehow manage to keep enough peace in the community that the preachers, teachers, missionaries, and evangelists would be spared life and limb for the preaching of the Gospel. We pray that God would keep order in the world through the application of simple justice. Then we cannot ask for special privilege for the preaching of the Gospel. Then we can only ask for what is fair and just for all men. That was the appeal of the town clerk. We can ask for no more. We are sorry that God does not win with all men; we wish that He might rule them by His Spirit and His love. But we pray that He might then at least rule them by law. Paul and his friends must have breathed a sigh of relief that they could go to bed safe that night. In their prayers they must have thanked God for His goodness. So often also we must express our gratitude for God's protection, though He may not have granted success as we would have liked to see it.

There is one more observation we can make about Paul's experience at Ephesus. We know how dedicated Paul was to the preaching of the Gospel of Jesus Christ. For him this meant that man was delivered from sin and death by what God has revealed in the death and resurrection of His Son

Jesus Christ. We learned that he was willing to challenge all the world to understand that there is no salvation in any other. He knew from his own experience what is meant to be delivered from bondage to sin and the Law. Christ was his Savior, and he was filled with zeal to preach that there was no salvation in any god that man could devise by his reason or his hands. Yet he also knew there was a time when men would reject his gospel. He had to leave Ephesus knowing that he had done his best. He was faithful to his commission. There was now a congregation at Ephesus, but he also knew that hostility in the city would always create tension for the church. Paul knew that our Lord Himself had said that there would be times when we must shake the dust off our feet and go into another place where men will readily and willingly accept the Gospel of His peace and grace. As heartbreaking as that may be, we also are realistic enough to understand how hardhearted men can be. God gave His own Son to die for the world, and even He did not earn either the gratitude or the affection of the world.

From this story we then can learn several things about how we have power in the midst of chaos. We need not be stampeded into believing that crisis necessarily and automatically spells doom for the church. We can learn that the church is not always going to be successful. We can learn that we can expect hostility from the world if we are going to encourage people to count the cost of the Gospel. But we must also carefully learn to keep cool under the pressure of a crisis. We must look carefully to see what is causing the crisis. We can expect God's good providence in our time of trouble and can look for His help, even from unexpected quarters. We can also learn to move on from a defeat to take up with new zeal the causes that our Lord may set before us. We need not subscribe for one moment to the thesis that there has to be a failure of the church in this generation. We are confident of God's power and mercy in creating and sustaining His church. He never leaves the church without power. Therefore we can assume—whatever He places on us by way of a burden—that we are to do what we know is essential to the cause of His Son Jesus Christ, our Lord.

power in the Gospel

For I am not ashamed of the Gospel: it is the power of God for salvation to everyone who has faith, to the Jew first and also to the Greek. For in it the righteousness of God is revealed through faith for faith; as it is written, "He who through faith is righteous shall live."

Romans 1:16-17

POWER in the Gospel

The distinguishing mark of the church, so we confess, is the Gospel of Jesus Christ, that is, the doctrine of justification by faith. We by no means infer that as a church body within Christendom that we have a monopoly on the Gospel or that we are the only ones who teach salvation by faith. That would be presumptuous indeed. It certainly would also run counter to our conviction, for we believe that wherever the Holy Spirit employs the Holy Scriptures, there He is able to and does bring men to faith. Further, as a group of Christians who do take the Scriptures seriously and do believe that the heart and soul of the Scripture is the Gospel, we maintain that everything we teach and preach – and the very life-style of the church – must be measured by the Gospel of Jesus Christ. We use the word "Gospel" in a variety of ways, but we mean by its narrow sense that a man is saved by the love of God which is in Jesus Christ. At present we should like to explore how this Gospel is a power among us and why we must use this Gospel as the very yardstick of the church's confession and life. We can do this on the basis of what the apostle Paul explained to the congregation at Rome when he spoke of the power of the Gospel.

Paul had a deep yearning to appear in the congregation at Rome, because he saw it as a key congregation in the program of the dispersion of the Gospel. Rome was the imperial city, the center of communications. It was the home of the military that had given the world the *pax Romana,* the Roman peace. As the capital of political and economic strategies, the decisions of Rome affected the lives of people all over the Mediterranean world. Apparently influential people could be expected to belong to the Christian congregation at Rome. Not all the converts were from among the poor and the uncultured. One could hope that the impact made upon this important congregation would redound to the success of many other efforts to spread the Gospel to new territories and areas. Paul is hopeful of this: If he can share His Gospel with Roman Christians, then he will greatly strengthen their position as a power among men. For this reason he writes to them in the most detailed way concerning the faith he holds and wants to share. The Epistle to Romans is Paul's dogmatics or formulated teachings in miniature. What we have in Romans is a carefully reasoned and well designed statement of what Paul counts essential to the faith.

Paul states at the very beginning of this letter that he is not ashamed of this Gospel, for "it is the power of God for salvation to everyone who has faith." It is a power for salvation, "for in it the righteousness of God is revealed." This is to say that it is the function of the Gospel to show us what God is really like. The Gospel is to remove all reason for disputing, guessing, or philosophizing about God. What men search for, either in the primitive forms of the tribal worship of idols or in the most sophisticated forms of reasoning or philosophizing about God, is of no avail. Men on their own cannot possibly find God or His righteousness. He must reveal Himself. He must tell us what He is like. Anything else will be a lie, a half-truth, a mistake, or an error. God Himself must speak loudly and clearly. That makes sense. It may not appear too sound to a generation of people who do not know exactly who they are or why they are. They may have to go to a psychiatrist or a psychologist to find out the nature of their own identity. But even then the therapist must learn from the individual his thoughts and emotions so that he can understand the person. So it is with God. The revelation of His true character cannot be left up to someone else. Only He can adequately and properly reveal to us what He is like. A description or a guess from someone else will not do.

God did reveal Himself clearly and fully in Jesus Christ. God became incarnate, that is, He took human form and flesh. As God had made man in His own image, in Jesus Christ God was made in the image of man. If we were to ask someone, "How can we know what God is like?" he might answer, "Look to man." However, while that answer is partially true, since man still has some knowledge of the God who created him above all other creatures and in His own likeness, man is so perverted by his fall into sin that he distorts the image of God so much that we could never know what God is like. But in Jesus Christ God can be known. In Him we can know what God is like because He is true man, perfect man. Because He is perfect man, He reveals perfectly the *imagio dei,* the image of God, for He is the very image of God. In Jesus Christ we then have the revelation of the true character and nature of God. From Him we learn what we need to know about God. We discover what we could know in no other way. In Him alone we discover what we can learn from nothing or no one else, because all else has been ruined and spoiled by man, who forfeited the image of God. But in Christ is the power of God unto salvation to every one who believes.

What is the righteousness which God has revealed in the Gospel of Jesus Christ? Most often we are apt to reduce the concept of righteousness only to "rightness," to being morally right. That is a temptation for us. We recall the temptation in the Garden and remember that the forbidden fruit was of the tree of "the knowledge of good and evil." We recall also that the claim of the Tempter was that if you taste of this fruit "you shall be as the gods." All of that sounds right to us. Why should not man be godly if he knows the difference between good and evil? Should not man be moral? Is he not good when he discerns between good and evil? But we must think a moment. Was it not the great sin of pride stemming from legalistic do's and don'ts that Jesus condemned in the Pharisees? Did not Luther protest vigorously against the legal and moral approach which the medieval church had superimposed upon the faith of the primitive church? Did not Paul fight against those who wanted to add legal restrictions to the Gospel? Why did these great figures take the stand they did? Does this mean that in this day of gross immorality we should not take a stand for morality? Not at all. What this does mean is that we cannot equate the righteousness of God with simple morality. The righteousness of God is something more. The righteousness of God is His being God, or if you will, Good.

There are many times when we know that God is dealing with us in a way that is totally strange to us. If we were God we would do otherwise, perhaps according to what we consider justice or morality. As Christians we accept what God is doing with us beyond our capacity to reason it out, believing that it will ultimately be for our best. How do we know this? Through Jesus Christ. In Him God demonstrated best His righteousness, even though this meant undeserved suffering, crucifixion, and death for Him. That did not appear to be justice. Yet is was. For in righteousness God acted on behalf of all His creatures, permitting His own Son to die for all. By this we know that our holy and righteous God does not act only by the Law. For if He had, we would all have to die eternally for our sins. But in Christ Jesus we know that He acts in love. In Him we discover that His true nature is that He is love. John says, "God is love." Righteousness then is God's perfect disposition toward us which He manifests in love that we may be right with Him. This righteousness is revealed that we might live in it and be restored to the image which we once lost by sin.

Paul says that this righteousness of God is "revealed through faith for faith; as it is written, 'He who through faith is righteous shall live.'" While God has left this clear and intelligible witness to His righteousness in Jesus Christ, the fact remains that it is not so obvious to everyone in the world. There are all kinds of people who stumble over this truth about God, who refuse to acknowledge it or see it. The natural man does have the power to refuse the things of God. And unfortunately that appears to be man's disposition. Only by faith can he see it and believe. In Matthew's Gospel Jesus said to His disciples, "Blessed are your eyes for they see, your ears for they hear" (13:16). Many times He concluded His teaching with the words, "He that has ears to hear let him hear." But sadly Jesus had to admit that many refused to believe. And to His disciples He said, "To you it has been given to know the secrets of the kingdom of heaven." (Matt. 13:11) That we acknowledge the truth and power of the Gospel, this is the work of the Spirit of God in us. God creates believers. Believers are not born of themselves. God must make believers of men by opening their eyes and ears and hearts to the revelation of His righteousness. The Gospel is a matter of faith. By faith we appropriate to ourselves the gift of righteousness which God gladly imputes to us by faith in Jesus Christ.

Righteousness is revealed through faith for faith. The one who shares the Gospel of Jesus Christ does so by faith. He believes the Gospel which has been transmitted to him by another believer in Jesus Christ. So Paul could trace his spiritual lineage back to Abraham, the believer according to promise. We can trace ours back to the apostle Paul. Now all of us who believe come under the great privilege of knowing the power of this Gospel, of which none of us should be ashamed. By faith we can see and hear the clear revelation of God's Gospel in Jesus Christ. Therefore we are capable of seeing something that others do not or will not see. We have the power to share, not because we are powerful of ourselves but because we live under the power and influence of God's Holy Spirit, and because the Gospel itself is a power unto salvation. The apostle was calling upon the Romans to be partners with Him in an enterprise that would endure long beyond the fall of Rome. He knew it would. He calls on us today to share in the same enterprise, because he knows that this power of God's love will endure whatever the crises of our days will be.

power *for Teaching*

So I ask you not to lose heart over what I am suffering for you, which is your glory.

For this reason I bow my knees before the Father, from whom every family in heaven and on earth is named, that according to the riches of His glory He may grant you to be strengthened with might through His Spirit in the inner man, and that Christ may dwell in your hearts through faith; that you, being rooted and grounded in love, may have power to comprehend with all the saints what is the breadth and length and height and depth, and to know the love of Christ which surpasses knowledge, that you may be filled with all the fullness of God.

Now to Him who by the power at work within us is able to do far more abundantly than all that we ask or think, to Him be glory in the church and in Christ Jesus to all generations, forever and ever. Amen.

Ephesians 3:13-21

POWER
for Teaching

In the church we must take seriously the task of educating. As we do so we are mindful of the role of the teacher. Our Sunday school and Bible class teachers are dedicated to being good teachers. But what is a good teacher? Children in the lower grades in school are apt to think that the best teacher is one who is good to them or does not expect too much from them. Those of us who are older remember as our best teachers those who demanded the most from us. It is worth noting that the eulogies for the late football coach Vince Lombardi centered on his demand for excellence from those who were his students on the football field. Any teacher who is recognized as teacher of the year in his field is very likely so honored because of what he demands of his students. Yet this is probably a poor way of saying it, because the teacher who demands much is really the one who gives the most. He gives of himself as he enters into the life and concerns of his students and follows through with them to the achievement of the goals in learning. So it is that as we look for the model in our teaching, we see that our Lord Himself as the great Teacher not only demands of us but gives of Himself for us. In giving Himself to us He gives us power for teaching.

When we go to school we should know why we are learning. That may sound foolish to the young schoolboy who cannot find any good reasons why he should be going to school. Yet the question stands behind every school system and educational enterprise. Teachers and educators debate the purposes and goals of a popular TV program like "Sesame Street" as well as the philosophy behind a graduate school in the finest of our universities. In recent years most of our education has been geared to helping prepare people for a vocation in life. We have made that so much our goal that most of education was highly specialized. Almost everything that students learned and did was designed to help them with their chosen occupation. The goal of education was to make the student a good engineer, a good nurse, a good teacher, a good chemist, a good musician, and the like. We worked so hard at this that at a university the school of engineering and the school of nursing were totally separated from one another. The language used in the different schools was so varied that the vocabulary of one school almost sounded like a foreign language to another school. We have become quite expert at making good graduates in each school, but we have not asked, "Have we made them good or better persons?"

Not only have we not asked if education should make for better people; we have not even asked if we have helped our students to understand the world around them. Have we helped them to understand themselves and the people around them? What a tragedy it is that we have amassed so much talent, learning and ability for our space program only to discover that there is so much marriage and family unhappiness and misery in the homes of the people associated with that program! As a campus pastor I saw that many students entered the university filled with prejudices and left the university four years later still filled with the same prejudices. Our problem is that we have become so intense about learning for vocation that we have not learned how to appreciate or use properly the world around us. Consequently we find that the present generation of students is raising serious questions about the world they live in. They accuse us of having failed in some critical issues that affect the use and management of the creation. They believe that the overriding questions of the day are not what kind of jobs they are going to have but the questions of war, racism, and ecology. This is an extremely interesting phenomenon. We are suddenly confronted with a whole generation of students who tell us about the gross failure of our educational system. It was bound to happen. How could we think that we could train people so thoroughly in their vocations that they would have to be blind and deaf to the major problems around them?

This is why our educational program is so important. What we do here is to seek to wrestle with the main questions in life. We know that each one will have to decide on and prepare for his profession in life in his own way according to the ability that God gives. But together we must deal with the questions that are common to us all. Our advantage in doing this together is to learn from the Creator Himself about the creation in which we live. The creation, the world, the atmosphere in which we live are a great mystery unless we know by whom and why they were created. These are answers not found in test tubes. They are revealed by God Himself in our Lord Jesus Christ. Here in our studies of His Word, our worship, and our working together we learn the secrets of the great universe. In Jesus Christ we learn that God created us for the purpose of serving one another in love. But we learn much more than that. We also learn that our Lord Jesus Christ Himself is the model for giving care to the universe. From Him we learn how we should act in the creation, and we also learn how we find the strength and the help for doing what is necessary and important.

All this means that we must learn more than just facts. The apostle prays, ". . . that you, being rooted and grounded in love, may have power to comprehend with all the saints, what is the breadth and length and height and depth, and to know the love of Christ which surpasses knowledge, that you may be filled with the fullness of God" (Eph. 3:17-19). So the chief aim of Christian education should be to know the love of Christ which goes far beyond knowledge. This was saying a great deal. For in the day in which this was written "knowledge" did not mean the accumulation of facts as we often now view knowledge. To the Greeks knowledge meant a definite view of the universe and the destiny of man. But the apostle knew that whatever men had reasoned out about the meaning of their life was surpassed by what Christians know in the Lord Jesus Christ. Paul saw that in the cross of the Lord Jesus Christ we come to understand the love of Christ. In Him love has no limits as to height, depth, breadth, and length. In Him we come to understand the nature of man's sin and also the nature of God's love. In Him we discover not only what the trouble with man is but also what the power of God's love is. In Him we learn about our own weakness, and we also find strength in Him. In Jesus we discover what the true value of life is and that we cannot limit ourselves to what is obvious to the eye or the ear.

This is important for us to talk about these days. Most of us who are parents today grew up in an educational system that worked with the scientific method. That method doubted anything that could not be established by experiment or clinical experience. That method called into question much of what we accept by faith. At the same time the method was always open to revision, that is to say: If we learned that some new discovery called into question an old truth, we promptly dropped the old. That system made all truth highly questionable and gave a great deal of insecurity to the world. Today we see how this has caused people to look for truth in strange places. Young and old have been exploring the occult and the ancient theories about the spirit world to find some kind of security. In the scientific era these people have been looking for something that surpasses knowledge. In Jesus Christ we know that love which does surpass knowledge and takes all the insecurity out of life and places us under the power and influence of God's love. In His love we are able to find the answers necessary for everyday living and for facing the future that leads to His eternity. We should not be one bit surprised that young people today feel cheated by an educational system that is so sterile that it has no room for the life of the spirit. We ought redouble our efforts to demonstrate to them that the life of the spirit is not the life of spiritism and occultism, but that the life of the Spirit is in the love of Jesus Christ.

It is interesting to note that one of the earliest laws on education in America, the Massachusetts Bay Colony school law of May 1642, kept in good order the priorities in education. The selectmen of every precinct were to see to it that all could read and had knowledge of the capital laws. Next, parents were required to teach and catechize their children in some orthodox catechism of religion at least once a week. Then parents would be required to see that their children learned some lawful occupation. Today we must keep our educational priorities straight. We believe that it is the obligation of all Christian parents to see to it that their children are trained in the basics and fundamentals of the Christian faith. This means that we must dedicate ourselves to a vigorous program of Christian education. We cannot treat lightly what we do in Sunday school classes. We have to develop a well-trained Sunday school staff. Our catechetical school is important. But we cannot quit there either. We must go beyond this and let our youth and adult programs keep pace with all other efforts we give to learning, in order that our conviction that the love of Christ, which surpasses knowledge, may truly take root and have effect in our lives.

We now have a generation of youngsters who grew up with television who may have spent more hours in front of a television screen than their parents have spent in their lifetime of schooling. This means that the TV tube as a teacher surpasses the power and influence of the teacher of the generation ago. Now the question is: Are we going to permit television to become the chief influence and power for imparting knowledge to all of us? Or are we going to permit the love of Christ to surpass all influences in our life to enable us to grow in the inner man, that we might live under the influence of God's love in Christ? We must rededicate ourselves to the proposition that the love of Christ is superior to everything and everyone in the world. We must dedicate our children and ourselves to something that God has already guaranteed and assured us in His Son, our Lord. And that is the fullness of His love. The kind of dedication we make will have good results, not to the degree that we do something on our own merit or by our own power. Strangely and paradoxically enough, we will experience blessings to the degree that we rely upon the love of Christ which surpasses knowledge.

power *in Prayer*

Continue steadfastly in prayer, being watchful in it with thanksgiving; and pray for us also, that God may open to us a door for the Word, to declare the mystery of Christ, on account of which I am in prison, that I may make it clear, as I ought to speak.

Colossians 4:2-4

POWER in Prayer

Many changes in agriculture and in our general economy have taken place since those medieval rogation days when the companies of the faithful marched out to the fields for the blessing of the fields. The simple acts of planting and sowing were matched with simple prayers acknowledging dependence on God's mercies. Today many hands are directly and indirectly involved in the business of producing, packaging, and marketing the blessings of God's creation. However, in spite of great advances in agriculture, half of the world's three billion people go to bed hungry each night. Experts estimate that we must double our food production in a short time if we are to deal effectively with the growing world food problem. When we couple this enormous task with the ecology and environmental problems, we must conclude that we are moving deeper and deeper into crises that engulf us all. We have become more obviously dependent upon one another. No matter what one's vocation, he is somehow tied into the business of carefully husbanding the world's resources. We especially as Christians, who accept the stewardship of life as a calling of God, must give ourselves to solution of the world's problems. But where do we begin? Our Lord gives us the promise of prayer. The apostle encourages us to begin with prayer. Let us begin by testing the power of prayer.

In his catalog of duties in the Epistle to the Colossians the apostle Paul says, "Continue steadfastly in prayer."

This means that we are to storm heaven with our prayers in the same way an army would lay stubborn siege to a city. God invites us to do so. The psalmist tells us that God says, "Try Me" (Ps. 139:23). The prophets urge Israel over and over again to bring the large problems of the nation to their waiting God. Our Lord encourages us to pray for all things. Luther stated it so simply and yet so powerfully, "Our Father . . . has commanded us so to pray and has promised to hear us." The Lord commands us to pray, making prayer a Christian duty. But the command is in itself a promise of blessing. God does not issue His command for self-satisfaction, but calls us to prayer that He might bless us by offering His aid to us. Prayer is the instrument which God gives to us, that His power and love might be available to us. We are to begin tackling any problem, crisis, or task with the invocation of God's blessing on what we must do.

The apostle does more than urge us to pray. He gives us some pointers on prayer. He says, "Continue steadfastly in prayer being watchful in it." What are we to watch for? Obviously he means that we should be watchful against temptation. He certainly does not mean that we should guard only against the larger crimes against society. But he means that prayer should be the helpful instrument by which we are kept aware of the constant pressures under which we live. Prayer is the alert system by which we keep tuned to the things that threaten our obedience to God. Prayer is the sensitizer to those situations which can jeopardize our relationship with God. By prayer we are able to see how every occasion in life is either a temptation or a test. Without prayer everything is a temptation by which we can dishonor God or do a disservice to our neighbor. With prayer we can see how the same occasion is a test by which God calls us to obedience and faithfulness. A prayerful approach to life is in reality a faithful approach to life – to a life in which by faith we see God's hand in all of life and that He is the Lord and Ruler of life. It is the function of prayer to let us see how God fits into our life situations and how we then must and should respond because of His presence. The mechanism of prayer is not as complicated as some people make it sound. Prayer is really the inner working of the Holy Spirit that goes on in spite of how inadequate we sometimes may feel about prayer.

Formulation of the words appears to be our chief difficulty with prayer. People are overawed by some who can put a lot of pretty words together, or who can offer lengthy prayers. Jesus says we are not to be intimidated by hypocrites who pray like that. He says they are no different than empty talkers, "for they think they will be heard for their many words." The effectiveness of prayer is not dependent on the words but on the attitude, the faith and the confidence in God's willingness to help. To those who think they do not know how to pray I offer the comfort of Paul, who says, "We do not know how to pray as we ought, but the Spirit Himself intercedes for us with sighs too deep for words" (Rom. 8:26). The rules for prayer are very simple: "Pray anywhere, any time, and any way." To "pray anywhere and any time" does not need explanation. But "pray any way" should not ignore the basic injunctions to pray in faith in our Lord Jesus Christ. "Pray any way" means pray in spite of what you think is your inability to pray. Pray in spite of your feeling unworthy to pray. Pray in spite of your hangups. Pray in spite of all of the hindrances you think there are to prayer. Pray in spite of the impossible situation in which you find yourself. Pray in spite of the fact that you think it is impossible for God to hear your prayer. Pray because God will hear you. Pray because God desires to help you.

The apostle adds more: "Continue steadfastly in prayer,

being watchful in it with thanksgiving." The matter of thanksgiving is important to the apostle. Thanksgiving is fundamental to worship. Thanksgiving is also essential to prayer. Thanksgiving is basic to prayer because to be thankful to God is to recall all that God has done for us. What God has done in the past for His children is the springboard for prayer. We have the examples of faith heroes in the Scriptures, but not one of them was heroic by virtue of his own power. All were dependent on the strength which they received from God through prayer. What is striking about the Biblical heroes is that they are such ordinary sinners. But they become extraordinary because God gives them power through prayer. As we recite the feats of those heroes, we know that we are telling stories of accomplishments of God through men who stretched themselves beyond the ordinary through prayer. That is cause for us to be thankful and hopeful. But we have yet better reason. The foundation for thankful prayer is what our God has done for us through our Lord Jesus Christ. Our Lord was the Man of Prayer. Not only was He exemplary in the way He spoke prayers, but His whole life was prayerful in the sense that He set Himself to doing the will of His Father. In prayerfully doing the will of the Father He accomplished our salvation, because by being watchful in prayer He submitted Himself to our death and our punishment. And when the Father raised Him from the dead, He gave answer to the prayer of His Son and thereby promised to answer all our prayers.

To be thankful for what our God has done for us in this Christ is to be aware of what He can do for us today. This is what Jesus is talking about when He says, "If you ask anything of the Father, He will give it to you in My name. Hitherto you have asked nothing in My name; ask, and you will receive that your joy may be full" (John 16:23-24). Jesus is saying that He is the assurance to us that the

Father will hear our prayers and answer them. Our Lord is the guarantor of our praying. To pray in His name is to pray with the confidence that God can and will do something for us no matter how grave the situation will be. To pray in His name is to pray with the absolute assurance that God knows what He is doing for us. To pray in His name is to increase our potential for service and for doing His will. To pray in His name is to pray with joy and fullness of heart. To pray in His name is to open to ourselves the possibility of all that God would have us do. Not to pray in Jesus' name is to neglect power. When we fail to pray thankfully we remain weak when we could be strong. To pray in Jesus' name is to discover what we can be when we count on God to help us.

Paul adds one more feature of prayer: "And pray for us also, that God may open to us a door for the Word, to declare the mystery of Christ, on account of which I am in prison, that I may make it clear as I ought to speak." Our prayer should be intercessory prayer, that is, prayer for others. Here Paul asks that the prayers of his readers be for the sake of the Gospel. He is encouraging the people to pray that world conditions may so shape themselves that the scope of the Gospel might be expanded. Luther held to that kind of view. He urged that Christians participate in world and community affairs in order to effect and maintain peace, so that the cause of the Gospel might go forward and that men might demonstrate the true love of God in Christ Jesus. Are we willing to pray for that today? How much do we pray for it? Or are the accusations which are hurled at the church today correct? Are we selfish and only turned in on ourselves? Some have suggested that the more doctrinal the church is, the less human it is. Or the more orthodox it is, the more heartless and detached it is from world concerns. That may appear to be an exaggerated and oversimplified judgment. But we must ask ourselves, "How much have we prayed about world affairs? How much have we prayed for our neighborhood? How much have we prayed for the poor? How much have we prayed about world hunger?" Is another of the accusations correct, namely, that the average churchgoer "has a self-centered preoccupation with saving his own soul?"

If we have left this kind of impression upon the world—and the observation is that we have left it particularly with the younger generation—then we should do everything we can to change that impression. Let us be frank about it. Would we be irritated with the apostle Paul because he landed in jail for the sake of the Gospel? Would we be saying that he pushed the whole civil rights thing too far in connection with his Roman citizenship? Or would we see that we were to become his partners in the Gospel through our faith and prayer? Today the call comes to us to begin with real and genuine prayer for all that troubles us in the world, to pray for the world, to pray for peace, to pray for the end of racial strife, to pray for an end to pollution, to pray for the hungry of the world, to pray for the poor, to pray for our enemies, to pray for the church. Today we are called to serve the world. We can ignore the call and do nothing if we are not men of prayer. But if this invitation to prayer means anything to us, let it mean this: We are determined to become intercessors for the world, that the cause of the Gospel might be advanced to the far corners of the earth.